ANOTHER

MONTH OF

SUNDAYS

DR. MALCOLM BURTON

RevMedia Publishing
PO Box 5172
Kingwood, TX 77325
www.revmediapublishing.com

ISBN-13: 978-1-7324922-8-8
Printed in the United States of America

1 2 3 4 5 6 7 8 9 10 11 21 20 19 18 17 16 15 14

CONTENTS

WHY I WROTE THIS BOOK

I Love People.

I have a grand obsession.
It is really a pretty simple one: Helping others succeed.
I don't mind studying for hours on end to gain a desired result.
Everything I write is believed to be from a Christian perspective.
As a result of this, my plan is to spend the rest of my life reminding people of their position in Christ. If we can keep this focus, success is inevitable.

> *"There are but two things worth living for: to do what is worthy of being written; and to write what is worthy of being read,"* —-Ross Perot.

Mr. Perot shared something I really believe.
This is why I keep living...and writing!

Malcolm Burton

Madison County, Texas
August 2019

CHAPTER ONE

Letting Go

Fresh Success Can Be Yours.

How? By consciously "letting go."
Releasing situations you can't change.
Yes, I'm still fighting some challenges, as you likely are.
But, I continue to sow faith for healing and miracles into others.
That is why I'm encouraged, "Whatever a man sows is what he will reap," (Galatians 6:7b).

I think a lot.
I've been wronged.
You have been wronged, too.
I will even confess to wronging others.
These are all things each of us must let go.

"Multitudes, multitudes in the valley of decision! For the day of the Lord is near in the valley of decision," (Joel 3:14).

This valley symbolizes God's vengeance.
Old Testament vengeance was violent retribution.
New Testament vengeance is God making things right for us.
It brings peace to my emotions to know that what I've done, and the things that have been done to me, have all been made right by the blood sacrifice of Jesus.
Letting go frees God to work for me.
The Holy Spirit is then free to right my wrongs.
I know He is righting the offense I've sown into others.
He is bringing possibility out of what appears to be lost.

He is restoring things stolen from me...*and from you, too.*

"But the Lord will be a shelter for His people, and the strength of the children of Israel," (Joel 3:16b).

Life seems to bring storms.
Let Him be your shelter and source of strength.
I'm discovering letting go to be a constant decision.
It serves as a preventative against unnecessary storms.
Please, let go of what hurts you. Cling to our Lord Jesus, The One Who Heals.

Life is better for those who choose to let go.
Especially when we let go...*and let God.*

CHAPTER TWO

Four Things Paul Knew

I Value Nothing More Than the Call of God.

For some reason, God chose me for His work.

I am not insecure, but I do know my human flaws.

My Mom attempted to pay tribute to me one Pastors Appreciation Day.

Teary eyed and emotional, Mom said, "If God can use my son... He can use anyone!"

I recognize my humanity and my need to have the enabling power of the Holy Spirit for the work of ministry.

1) Paul Understood His Assignment.

> *"Paul, an apostle (not from men nor through man, but through Jesus Christ and God the Father who raised Him from the dead)," (Galatians 1:1 NKJV).*

Accountability is a necessary thing.

The call of God is a strange and mystic thing.

It is mysterious, but clearly observable when working in people.

The power of God is a thing that enables people to do supernatural things.

Paul understood his ultimate accountability was to the God who called him.

These supernatural gifts cannot consistently and correctly be operated by believers without accountability.

Paul knew He would stand before a holy God who would hold

Him accountable for His works. And, yes, Mom inadvertently brought the house down with laughter that great day.

2) Paul Knew the Value of Working With Others.

Galatians 1:2, "...and all the brethren who are with me,"

Paul was a team builder.
He constantly worked with others.
When young, he was mentored by older men.
This wasn't always a good thing. Paul, then known as Saul, was observed holding the coats of the men who stoned Evangelist Stephen.
Thank God we do get another chance to make things right. As an older man, Paul was found busily mentoring others.

3) Paul Knew God Had Called Him To Serve Particular Groups Of People.

"To the churches of Galatia:" (Vs 2B)

We are not called to everyone.
However, we are all called to someone.
Paul focused his attention upon identifying those who would receive his ministry.

4) Paul Knew the Power of the Grace of God.

"Grace to you and peace from God the Father and our Lord Jesus Christ," (Vs 3).

Proper teaching of grace holds believers accountable.
Contrary to my youthful teaching, grace is not a license to sin.
Grace enables flawed people to serve a holy God in an unholy world.
You actually have the power within for a successful life.
Your successful life is lived out day-by-day.
Move in grace today...and every day.

CHAPTER THREE

We've Been Delivered

Paul Had Many Admirable Traits.

A towering intellect, Paul came to value spiritual things more.
It is clear Paul enjoyed cerebral challenges, but he appreciated the revelation brought his way by the Holy Spirit much more than what was produced by his own thoughts.
He was a man who walked in victory, but understood life brought trials.

Three Admirable Traits of Paul

1) Paul Knew He Had Been Delivered from The Powers of Hell.

> *"...who gave Himself for our sins, that He might deliver us from this present evil age," (Galatians 1:4A)*

Christianity is not just another philosophy.
Christianity is to be a reflection of the ability of God.
Our Lord is not cowering in fear before demon spirits today.
He is victorious over them, and Paul teaches that we are to be victorious over them, too.

2) Paul Knew That Victory Was the Will Of God For His Life.

> *"...according to the will of our God and Father," (Galatians 1:4B).*

I tell this story repeatedly.
Plum Grove Assembly holds fond memories for me.
One standard greeting was, "Have you got the victory today?"

Paul knew the will of God for His life was victory over sin and all the works of satan.

God does not want us drifting through life while struggling in mediocrity and fear of evil works.

Jesus paid the full price for us to live in total victory over all the potential issues of life.

3) Paul Was Quick to Glorify God for The Good Things in His Life.

"...to whom be glory forever and ever. Amen," (Galatians 1:5).

We all have abilities.

We have no abilities that did not originate in Him.

Paul saw himself as someone made more than a conqueror.

As noted earlier, it is abundantly clear to me that Paul knew he was an exceptionally gifted person.

However, it does not take much examination to see Paul constantly offering glory to the Lord.

My prayer today is that we may cultivate a lifestyle of appreciation and voiced thanksgiving for the goodness of our Lord God.

CHAPTER FOUR

Restoration of Others and Self-Examination

Paul Exhorted Us to Do Something.

This "something" is an action few seem to consider.
Paul exhorted us to move to restore the fallen believer.
He encouraged us to restore the broken without judging him, or her.
By doing such we heal the broken and protect ourselves from a hellish harvest.

> *"Brethren, if a man is overtaken in any trespass, you who are spiritual restore such a one in a spirit of gentleness," (Galatians 6:1).*

Restoration is spiritual.
Plainly put, judgment is not spiritual.
Judgment creates problems for all concerned.
I have seen fallen Christians be treated poorly after their collapse.
It has not often been my experience that the broken have been abused by unbelievers. Instead, they were tormented by The Church.

> *"...considering yourself lest you also be tempted...." (1B).*

As I write, I am thinking of one of the most well-known Evangelists of my lifetime.
In 1985 ABC News surveyed 1100 people in "man on the street" interviews by showing a series of photos. These individuals were surveyed to see if they could name the individuals in the pictures.

This particular Evangelist was the second most well-known individual in the United States, trailing only then President Ronald Reagan.

More people identified this Full-Gospel preacher than correctly recognized the man who would become the next President of the United States, George Herbert Walker Bush.

"But let each one examine his own work, and then he will have rejoicing in himself alone, and not in another," (Galatians 6:4A).

It is time to narrow our focus.

Instead of evaluating other lives, we should consider our own.

"For each one shall bear his own load," (Galatians 6:5)

This is a double reference verse.

We must engage in personal responsibility.

We are to clearly consider the pathway we walk.

Yet, Paul exhorts us to restore the fallen believer to wholeness.

When we do so we make sure we do not fall ourselves.

CHAPTER FIVE

Shock and Surprise

I'm Opposed to Predestination.

I believe it is a flawed doctrine that hinders many.

Instead of assuming responsibility for their life, many believers blame God.

They have been taught, incorrectly, everything that happens here on earth is the will of God.

When I shared this thought online, it made a friend smile.

I entitled it, *"Shock and Surprise: I Believe in Predestination."*

My Presbyterian minister friend claimed it made him shout for joy.

He read the title and claims to have thought, "Wow! I converted Malc!"

But, no one should really get carried away because I have a "qualified" thought about predestination.

> *"Blessed be the God and Father of our Lord Jesus Christ, who has blessed us with every spiritual blessing in the heavenly places in Christ, 5 having predestined us to adoption as sons by Jesus Christ to Himself, according to the good pleasure of His will," (Ephesians 1:4-5).*

We are already blessed.

Not looking to be blessed in the future...*although we will be.*

The blessings of God are already ours...*available to us today!*

These blessings flow from God the Father and our Lord Jesus through the Holy Spirit.

The things we need exist in both this natural realm and the spirit realm.

All the blessings of God are appropriated by faith.
And (...take a deep breath) are already ours.
They've been given to us.
They're already ours.
Right now.

> *"...just as He chose us in Him before the foundation of*
> *the world, that we should be holy and without blame*
> *before Him in love," (Ephesians 1:4).*

The Bible does teach predestination of events.
Personal salvation is certainly not one of those predestined events.
Before the earth was created, Jesus decided to choose anyone who received Him.
It is predestined that the born again, both living and dead, will rise to eternally be with Him.

Let me paraphrase what Jesus said, "Whoever will choose to do so may come unto Me and I will not turn him away."

> *"to the praise of the glory of His grace, by which He made*
> *us accepted in the Beloved," (Ephesians 1:6).*

His grace is another attribute that qualifies Him for glory.
We have done nothing to deserve this grace, but He gives it to anyone who will receive.
I cannot be moved away from this fact...*the church is predestined to display the glory of God.*
I am part of that church. His glory will be manifest through me.

After all, it is predestined.

Go on. Smile. I am.

CHAPTER SIX

Relationship Thoughts

Ministers Are Always On Duty.

Angie is a manager at one of my favorite restaurants.

I love the entire Pappas Brothers Restaurant chain, but The Pappadeaux Cajun Restaurant is a personal favorite.

Some very dear friends took me out to Pappadeaux for a birthday celebration.

I live by the theory that I am the Pastor of an area. I serve both the saved and unsaved.

No, I'm not the only Pastor in the area, but one of the Pastors set here to do marketplace ministry.

Because of this motivation, it was while out with friends that a series of conversations was started with Angie that still continue.

Seeing me interact with my adult children when visiting the restaurant caused Angie to seek out my opinions on parenting.

A little humor often helps open the door to conversation. So, I shared:

Five Things My Father NEVER Said...

1) "Your Mom and I are going out of town for the weekend. Why don't you invite some friends over for a party?

2) "Of course I would like to co-sign for your loan on a Corvette!

3) "You cannot continue to live under my roof unless you get a tattoo.

4) "Sure you can find a girl anyone would want to marry in a place like that.

5) "You don't have enough money for earrings? Here's another $100...get your nose pierced, too!"

I love being a Dad.
I am thankful for my Dad.
I am thankful I am a Dad.
Yes, life has challenges aplenty.
But the joy of relationship makes it all better.
My children are remarkable, but they have all had challenges.
The example my parents set by walking with me through my challenges helped me to walk with them.
Maybe someone in your family is challenged today. Instead of rejecting them, pray for them and ask God how you can help.

Everyone I know has needed help at some point.
Your loving attention may be all they need.
You will help them get over their hump.

CHAPTER SEVEN

Seven Relationship Related Truths

I Love People.

I define my life by relationships.
I know that trait is primarily feminine.
Yet, it is true of decidedly masculine Malc.
If my relationships are going well, I'm usually happy.

1) Learn and Remember the Word of God. "My son, do not forget my law," (Proverbs 3:1)
Relationships are the joy of my life.
Relationships are the greatest challenge of my life.
Relationships can only be maximized when they are built on the Word of God.

2) Let The Word of God Keep Your Heart. "But let your heart keep my commands; (Proverbs 3:1B).
The Word of God is above everything.
We need the Word to keep our lives balanced.
Relationships can never be allowed to become a substitute for the Word of God.
Relationships contain an ebb and flow element that can only be balanced by the constancy of the Word of God.

3) Reap The Reward of Obedience. "For length of days and long life, and peace they will add to you," (Proverbs 3:2).
Please say this aloud, "The Word of God is a life-giver."
Stress is a joy-robbing thief that can shorten the lives of those who do not learn how to manage it.

Please do yourself a favor by declaring these words aloud, too, "The Word of God releases the peace necessary to lengthen my life-span."

4) Be Merciful...Even with Those Who Don't Deserve Such. "Let not mercy and truth forsake you; Bind them around your neck, Write them on the tablet of your heart," (Proverbs 3:3).

I make the choice to live in mercy today.

I will not forsake the principle that one who has been forgiven much is required to forgive much.

I have been forgiven "much" and choose to freely recall this principle because it is written within the confines of my heart.

5) Live in The Favor Brought About by Obeying the Word of God. "And so find favor and high esteem in the sight of God and man," (Proverbs 3:4).

Honor is an incredible force.

Favor is released as we obey God's Word.

When we live in a manner that blesses others, honor is routed our way.

6) Place The Totality of Your Trust in The Right Person. "Trust in the LORD with all your heart, And lean not on your own understanding;" (Proverbs 3:5).

People will disappoint you.

Those you're intimately involved with may fail you

But, this is no reason to routinely cast people aside each time they stumble in the relationship.

Choose to forgive and believe God will help move your interaction forward into better things.

Choose to be a minister of reconciliation and restoration.

7) Acknowledge The Goodness of God Each Time It Manifests. "In all your ways acknowledge Him, And He shall direct your paths," (Proverbs 3:6).

God desires to guide His people into good things.

More good things are released each time we acknowledge

God's blessing.

My prayer for my reader is that you enjoy this special day. Special day? Yes, the Lord made it (Psalm 118:24). Rejoice and be glad in it.

"Relationships can only be maximized when they are ordered built on the Word of God,"

—MALC BURTON

CHAPTER EIGHT

Stepping into Victory

"Have You Got the Victory Today?"

Yes, that question still echoes in my memory.

Even today it is a thought that still runs through my mind, and is a question I ask myself.

The Apostle Paul openly and ardently encouraged us, his readers, to make sure we are living in faith rather than blithely going along.

The question posed above should provoke thought. My prayer is that it will cause us to grasp this important truth: *Being a Christian is sharply different from living life as a victorious believer.*

Having a home in heaven differs from living in victory on earth.
Please ponder these keys to living in victory.

1) Knowing The Will of God for Your Life.

"Paul, called to be an apostle of Jesus Christ through the will of God, and Sosthenes our brother," (1 Corinthians 1:1).

Paul was a Christian first, last and always.

But, Paul was also very conscious of his leadership role in the church.

Yes, he was a man who moved in revelation, a large part of that understanding concerned his role as an Apostle.

Paul was sent by the Holy Spirit to serve as The Apostle of the Gentiles.

Paul conducted missionary campaigns, established churches and created leadership teams to direct each group.

Clearly, Paul understood the will of God for his life.

2) Living in Sanctification. "To the church of God which is at Corinth, to those who are sanctified in Christ Jesus, called to be saints, with all who in every place call on the name of Jesus Christ our Lord, both theirs and ours:" (1 Corinthians 1:2).

Sanctification, in this context, refers to someone who has been set aside for God's special use and purpose.

Each believer, in another element of this gift of grace, is not to just seek God's sanctification for purification from the things of the flesh.

Each Christian is to seek to discover his/her individual area of service in the Kingdom of God and become sanctified in singular focus upon this calling.

3) Walking in Grace.

"Grace to you and peace from God our Father and the Lord Jesus Christ," (1 Corinthians 1:3).

In the universal sense, grace is the unmerited favor of God.

In this specific sense, grace is the Divine enabling to live a life of peace and productivity.

4) Living in Thanksgiving.

"I thank my God always concerning you for the grace of God which was given to you by Christ Jesus," (1 Corinthians 1:4).

We can never take our salvation for granted.

I am certain I am going to heaven and that will not change.

However, this can never be allowed to become a state of grace-filled living for which I am unthankful.

5) Receiving His Anointing to Testify for Him.

"...that you were enriched in everything by Him in all utterance and all knowledge," (1 Corinthians 1:5).

Yes, there are utterance gifts of the Holy Spirit.

But I also believe this is a promise of a more generic manner.

In addition to the manifestation gifts of the Holy Spirit, God gives each individual believer the utterance ability necessary to testify.

Not only do you receive overcoming power each time you testify,

others are drawn to God by your words.
Your testimony is a big deal.
It is an important part of effective Christianity.
Work on, practice giving your testimony. Refine it.
Paul never tired of sharing his testimony.
We can't afford to tire of sharing ours.
Lives are hanging in the balance.

"People warn you to never go off course. While that is good advice, it is also impossible. People do make mistakes. Wise people realize when they have made a mistake, and quickly do what is necessary to get back on course."

—Dr. Oral Roberts

"And they overcame him by the blood of the Lamb and by the word of their testimony, and they did not love their lives to the death" (Revelation 12:1)

Chapter Nine

Five More Keys to Living in Victory

God is "For" Us.

We are His special people.
He desires that we live in His best.
Even if desired, this victory is not an automatic.
There are things we must learn to be effective for Him.

1) Expect The Testimony of God to Be Confirmed in Your Life. "even as the testimony of Christ was confirmed in you," (1 Corinthians 1:6).

Yes, I am to "say" I have been changed.
 The initial change takes place inside the convert. Above all, the believer must live a life that reveals change. We are not just to testify to our changed heart. We are to demonstrate the fruits of righteousness that prove a changed life.

2) Receive The Gifts God Has for You. "so that you come short in no gift, eagerly waiting for the revelation of our Lord Jesus Christ," (Vs 7).

 The Holy Spirit is a giver of gifts. Each of His spiritual gifts have a common element...*revealing Jesus.*

3) Live A Blameless Lifestyle. "who will also confirm you to the end, that you may be blameless in the day of our Lord Jesus Christ," (8).

All believers will stand before God in judgment.

We will not be standing before Him for the determination of our salvation. We will, however, be standing before our God for the giving of rewards. Do not kid yourself. This will be important to you.

4) Depend Upon the Faithfulness of God.
"God is faithful,," (Vs 9).

Our God can be depended upon.
He can be trusted above all people.

5) Enjoy Fellowship with Him. "by whom you were called into the fellowship of His Son, Jesus Christ our Lord," (9B) .

God does not just love you. God also likes you...*and wants to spend time with you.*

Constantly increasing in my knowledge of Him is one of the best things about my life. My daily focus is to grow in relationship with and knowledge of Him.

Reach out to know Him in a fresh way today.

You will not regret your effort.

CHAPTER 10

Choose Not to Be Dismayed

Jahaziel.

I Didn't Remember His Name.

Yet, I have recalled his words for a long time.

He was a priest, but Jahaziel seems to have been no one significant at the time when God famously used him. "Then the Spirit of the Lord came upon Jahaziel..." (2 Chronicles 20:14).

Israel was in a mess.

Opposing forces had them outmanned.

An army may be (or may have been) facing you.

But there was no natural solution. I understand how that feels and you probably feel, or have felt, that way, too.

But a bold instruction came, and Jahaziel spoke it forth, "Listen, all you of Judah and you inhabitants of Jerusalem, and you, King Jehoshaphat! Thus says the Lord to you: 'Do not be afraid nor dismayed because of this great multitude, for the battle is not yours, but God's," (Vs 15).

Jehoshaphat was a great king.

He was a man Scripture finds blameless.

The son of King Asa, he followed God as his father had. Yet, as morally good and spiritually correct as Jehoshaphat was, He "hit the wall."

He didn't know what to do.

He had no sense of direction.

Then the prophetic directive flowed...*through someone else.*

> *"Tomorrow go down against them. They will surely come up by the Ascent of Ziz, and you will find them at the end of the brook before the Wilderness of Jeruel. 17 You will not need to fight in this battle. Position yourselves," (Vss 16-17).*

It's not always our fight. It is not always my turn to speak. Yet, I always want to "do something."

I am seldom thrilled with intercession. I am never happy about the idea of waiting. After all, my self-pejorative is "Microwave Malc". I want it now. Yet, there are times when there is little we can do but stand in faith.

Actually, there is nothing negative about doing all we can do and then standing in faith. The most powerful action we can take is always that of using our faith.

Like Jahaziel's command, we must "...stand still and see the salvation of the Lord, who is with you, O Judah and Jerusalem!'"

When little seems to be happening, He is with us. Our role is to believe and speak aloud His promises.

"Do not fear or be dismayed; tomorrow go out against them, for the Lord is with you." (Vs 17).

Today, don't fear.
Choose not to be dismayed.
Allow these verses to activate your faith.
The Holy Spirit knows the place and situation you're in.

He is not observing from afar. Like Jahaziel reminded King Jehoshaphat, "...the Lord is with you!"

You're too busy winning to consider quitting.
Speak to that mountain one more time.

Look! I see it moving!

"Speak to your mountain again. Look! I see it moving!"

—Malc Burton

CHAPTER 11

Lessons from an Overcomer

Lee Iacocca...

He died at age 94.
He knew great success and pain.
He created the iconic Ford Mustang.
He also birthed the ahead of its time Pinto.
He was fired as President of Ford Motor Company.
Why? Henry Ford II hated, "Uppity, Italian loudmouths."

Instead of allowing himself to be a victim of prejudice, Iacocca took the Chrysler Corporation from bankruptcy to profitability.

He changed my life with the statement, "I promise to do my very best. After all, what else is there?"

When I was 10-years-of-age I was described by a detractor as a "River Rat" from Plum Grove, Texas. As a young adult I observed Iacocca's example of strategic thought and followed that path out of poverty into success.

We never met, but I'll always appreciate the concepts of visionary thinking he stirred within me. His writings on leadership remain viable to this day. This is the very best I can do for his memory.

Maybe I can inspire someone today.

After all, what else is there?

Evangelist Oral Roberts was asked what would he do if the Board of Regents of the university he founded was to fire him. He said, "I would take my anointing to another place and be successful there!"

CHAPTER 12

Thoughts from A Faith Hero

Morning Prayer Time.

It is my Bible study time, too.
John Wesley is someone I value.
He shaped most of what I believe.
Of all historic figures, Wesley is my hero.
Yet, he was not a man immune to life's struggles.

Wesley did not understand relationship with God for much of his early life.

> *"I shall not be so bad as your other children. I will pray, read my Bible and go to church every day,"–John Wesley's response to Susanna Wesley's question of what qualified him for heaven.*

I didn't understand, either. All the things Wesley stated are good. Yet, they are not substitutes for salvation. Jesus said we must be born again, and that's the bottom line.

It is common for me to use *Wesley's Explanatory Notes* during my study. Wesley did not give up his search until he had a powerful experience with God. Each time I read his notes I'm thankful he shook off religious thinking and embraced the power of the Holy Spirit. From that moment forward his ministry shook the world. Religious thinking will cause you to criticize yourself. You will have a hard time looking outward to help others.

Religious thinking will make you shift your focus to rules.

I know because I've lived in that morass.

I have no intention of going back there.

I've breathed the clean air of grace. Life is too good here to be polluted.

Not again. Not ever.

Chapter 13

Surrounded by Champions

My life is filled with great people.
People who care enough to question.
They have moved from lack to manifest blessing.

> *"Constant Lack Is An Indicator of Disorder,"---Malc Burton.*

> *"Good understanding gives favor, but the way of the transgressor is hard," (Proverbs 13:15).*

My life changed when I questioned poverty. Yes, I've sown and worked, but I have unusual favor. The one single impartation I will never trade for anything else is favor.

Victory came to me years ago when Mike Murdock said, "You can gain more through one moment of favor than 1,000 days of labor."

I believed him.
I chose favor that night.
I began sowing favor into others.
I began calling God's favor into my life.
I still choose to walk the pathway of favor daily.
I'm looking for the next segment of Favor Highway...*now!*

> *"Show me your road, Lord Jehovah, and I shall walk in the truth; my heart shall rejoice with those who are in awe of your Name," (Psalms 86:15, The Aramaic Bible In Plain English).*

My life changed when I questioned.
My questions led me from error into truth.
Yes, I've struggled, but I'm still on my way through.
My life permanently modified when I walked out on religion.
When I embraced the potential of relationship, it was all over.

Define success as you wish, it is mine today.
Please, make your own bold declaration.
Walk on Favor Highway with me.

CHAPTER 14

Sent to Bless You

Jesus Came to Bless.

He did not come to judge.
The Father sent Him as salvation.
We know this sending was successful.
How? By the grace we've received from Jesus.

> *"To you first, God, having raised up His servant Jesus, sent Him to bless you, in turning every one of you from your iniquities," (Acts 3:26).*

Sin is missing the target.
Iniquity doesn't believe there is a target.
The Iniquitous Individual lives completely for "self".

God "raised up" Jesus as a servant to serve the needs of others. We have been "raised up" to serve, too. When we serve others we qualify for promotion in the Kingdom. We have received the blessing of salvation.

I am continually conscious of where I've come from.
My challenge is to remain focused on where I am going.

Jesus has blessed us with Holy Spirit power to serve in the Kingdom. There is a target in my life. I want to produce Kingdom fruit. Simple as it may seem, my aim is pleasing Him.

My goal is to live an inspirational life.

Every day...including today.

Make this choice with me!

CHAPTER 15

A Memorable Message

God Was Always Angry.

He was constantly vindictive.
God was looking to "get" people.
That was the posture of one family branch.
They thought they were the only real believers on earth.
Their God was one who felt mankind lived in constant failure.

As a boy, I remember despising family reunions because of the conflict that always erupted. My side was legalistic, too. But we were not guilty of thinking we were "it." We did not believe we were the only ones "saved".

My 16th year was life changing. During that season I started meeting people of positive faith such as Ron and Carolyn Smith, Clarence Dalrymple, John and Dodie Osteen and a quiet lady named Merle.

The Osteen's are legendary.

Clarence was (and remains) a powerful influence.

Those who know me have heard tales of how The Smiths impacted my life and shaped my ministry. But, as I write, I'm remembering Merle. I'm embarrassed to say I don't recall her family name, but I have never forgotten her message.

She introduced herself and said, "The Lord says Jeremiah 29:11 will be one of the most important verses of your lifetime."

She was absolutely correct, "For I know the thoughts that I think toward you, says the Lord, thoughts of peace and not of evil, to give you a future and a hope."

I'm glad I met The Loving God. I'm thrilled to serve the God of grace. I'm thankful I know the God of great patience. I'm ecstatic I know the God of power and demonstration. Yet, I'm also glad I met a lady named Merle who imparted truth.

Three Guiding Principles

1). God's thoughts toward me are good.

2). His plan for me is to have a desirable future.

3). My world of faith springs forth from daring to hope.

I'm on God's mind. You are in His thoughts, too. He is waiting on our faith words.

Say aloud, "Surely there is a future and my hope will not be cut off," (Proverbs 23:18).

You may be struggling. I'm looking for a way "out", too. Yet, the answer is already inside me. Let me share it so it can become your answer, too.

> *Job 22:28, "You will also declare a thing, and it shall be established for you."*

My faith is established. I believe yours is established, too. Join me in "declaring a thing." We'll see God establish it.

CHAPTER 16

Refocused and Ready

Focus Breakers Abound.

They come in all shapes and sizes.
They are people, events, circumstances and choices.
They are something very serious that must be dealt with.

> *Psalm 123:1, "Unto You I lift up my eyes, O You who dwell in the heavens."*

Dealing with needs is part of my life. Dealing with my own needs is a challenge, too. Absorbing and moving beyond the opinions of others is necessary. The opinions of others, both well-meaning and obviously negative, can be difficult to deal with.

Both require us to deliberately refocus our attention upon Jesus and His will for us as individuals and members of the corporate body known today as the church.

"Behold, as the eyes of servants look to the hand of their masters, as the eyes of a maid to the hand of her mistress, So our eyes look to the LORD our God, until He has mercy on us," (Vs 2).

John Wimber lived an amazing life.
He was the founder of The Righteous Brothers.
While playing keyboards for The Paramours, John met Jesus.

He was born again in the Quaker Church and led thousands to Jesus. Over time, John became quite dissatisfied with a focus breaker: *the lack of miracles in the church compared to the claims of The Bible.*

John asked the church leadership how they felt about the miracles of the Bible and was shocked by their response. They believed the miracles should be "discussed" but they did not really believe they were "for today"...focus breaker!

Instead of disregarding all of sacred writ, John Wimber got busy comparing scripture to scripture, allowing it to explain itself. He founded the Vineyard Fellowship Churches and became a minister of miracles because he chose to refocus.

You may be facing challenges today. Instead of throwing up my hands and walking away, I choose to refocus. My focus upon the call of God will not be broken. Instead, I declare that my focus will intensify.

I believe yours will, too.

CHAPTER 17

Four Facts About the Spirit-Filled Life

All Early Churches Were Spirit-Filled.

Pentecost Sunday is the birthday of the Church.
No, it is not the day the Spirit-Filled Church was born.
It is the birthday of the Church...period.
What do we mean by the term "Spirit-filled?"

We are describing those born again believers who have received Spirit-Baptism. While I know this is not a theological position to which all churches hold, I believe it to be the Biblical standard.

The initial evidence of Spirit-Baptism is speaking in a language unknown to the speaker.

Full Gospel believers are still being falsely accused of teaching that people must "speak in tongues" in order to be saved. We do not, and never have, believed such a bad and potentially destructive doctrine.

Spirit-Baptism is The Promise of The Father.

We, like the disciples of old, after we experience salvation are commanded to seek the "Promise of The Father."

> *"And being assembled together with them, He commanded them not to depart from Jerusalem, but to wait for the Promise of the Father, "Which," He said, "you have heard*

from Me; 5 for John truly baptized with water, but you shall be baptized with the Holy Spirit not many days from now."6 Therefore, when they had come together, they asked Him, saying, "Lord, will You at this time restore the kingdom to Israel?" 7 And He said to them, "It is not for you to know times or seasons which the Father has put in His own authority. 8 But you shall receive power when the Holy Spirit has come upon you; and you shall be witnesses to Me in Jerusalem, and in all Judea and Samaria, and to the end of the earth," (Acts 1:4-8).

God is always moving His people into a deeper relationship with Him (vs 5).

Someone will always object to the move of God in your life (vs 6). The Bible reveals how God always clarifies the thought process of those who really desire Him to do such (vs 7). God wants to empower us to witness for Jesus.

Spirit Baptism Is an Experience That Opens the Supernatural Realm.

"When the Day of Pentecost had fully come, they were all with one accord in one place. 2 And suddenly there came a sound from heaven, as of a rushing mighty wind, and it filled the whole house where they were sitting. 3 Then there appeared to them divided tongues, as of fire, and one sat upon each of them. 4 And they were all filled with the Holy Spirit and began to speak with other tongues, as the Spirit gave them utterance," (Acts 2:1-4).

God has always moved and done things in particular seasons (1A).

Unity is essential. I understand and desire this more than ever (1B).

The Full-Gospel Church has a particular sound (2). A "rushing mighty wind" is symbolic of God's urgent desire to meet the needs of His people.

We are the spiritual house where God dwells. God desires to fill the "whole house."

The fire of God's holiness falls upon us in a sanctifying way. We come to understand the critical importance of Him being number one.

What is the proof of Holy Spirit's activity? James calls the tongue the "most unruly member" of the body. Giving your tongue over to God for His glory is proof of a supernatural experience with Him.

Spirit Baptism Evokes an Eternal Question.

"So they were all amazed and perplexed, saying to one another, "Whatever could this mean?" 13 Others mocking said, "They are full of new wine." (Acts 2:12-13)

I have no problem with those who ask, "What is this about?" I will always do my best to explain what I believe. I will not waste time on disrespectful people.

Clarifying the Purpose of Spirit Baptism

"But you shall receive power when the Holy Spirit has come upon you; and you shall be witnesses to Me in Jerusalem, and in all Judea and Samaria, and to the end of the earth,"(Acts 1:4).

The point of receiving Spirit Baptism is receiving the power of God. We are to be actively involved in ministering miracles to those in need.

The late R.W. Schambach told of hearing Evangelist T.L. Osborn make what was a life-changing statement for him, "Those who cannot demonstrate the power of the Gospel have no right to preach the Gospel."

Words are not enough.

We are to be a people of signs, wonders and miracles.

Let's agree that we will consciously celebrate the move of the Holy Spirit in the Earth.

CHAPTER 18

We Open Dimensions by Words

We Open Both Good and Bad.

Good Dimensions and Evil Dimensions.

> *"Let us draw near to God here," (2 Samuel 14:33D).*

In the midst of daily activity Samuel opened a fresh move of the Holy Spirit by declaring, "Let us draw near to God here."

When we are in this place of close communication with God we have an opportunity to move even closer. This can be a special time when we let go of things, known and unknown, that hinder us. Things happen in the presence of God that don't happen anywhere else.

Most Christians are willing to give over to God for destruction the parts of their life they despise or consider worthless. (1 Samuel 15:9).

In all candor, there often seem to be secret things many believers do not really want to move away from.

When we make the decision to really do things God's way we are released into the blessing of Abraham. The Bible reveals in Romans 4:3, "Abraham believed God and it was accounted to him as righteousness." Everything we need is in our position of righteousness.

Just as we moved into this supernatural right standing by the exercise of faith, we manifest the blessings of righteousness by faith, too.

"How" we do things is important to God.

Establishing the Great Temple was a big deal. In 2 Samuel 7 we see God revealing the plan to Solomon.

When the Pattern is Right the Glory Will Fall

I have a Pentecostal background, for which I am very thankful.

My forefathers paid quite a price to preach and defend the doctrine that the Baptism in the Spirit and speaking in tongues is still for today. One of my contributions to this pattern is taking nothing away from their accomplishments, but to add all I can. I owe their efforts and legacy this continued faithful activity.

Having said that, I also owe it to the people to whom I minister to clarify the wrong conclusions too many have about Holy Spirit baptism. Spirit Baptism is not tongues for the sake of tongues. Praying in tongues is a powerful gift that opens great revelation.

It is this release of power that causes me to recommend this experience to all believers who desire to go deeper. This outpouring is important and available to everyone. However, once again, it is not about tongues. It is for the release of God's supernatural ability into the life of the individual using this gift through prayer.

And it's not just power for miracles.

It's so that the power-charged atmosphere of Heaven can rest upon a person in such a way that it causes a shift in the atmosphere over a home, business, or city.

Pray in the spirit today.

Make the decision to linger a little longer.

We are always better when we are in the God's presence.

This is especially so when we honor Him by speaking in the supernatural language He gives all believers.

"Make the decision to linger a little longer. We are always better when we are in God's presence,"

—MALC BURTON

CHAPTER 19

Properly Placed Confidence

I Am a Confident Person.

I am confident of my gifting.
I understand the call of God upon my life.
But, I am not self-reliant. My trust in is in the Lord.

> *"Therefore let him who thinks he stands take heed lest he fall," (1 Corinthians 10:12).*

Yes, you should be self-confident. However, self-sufficiency guarantees a fall. Be confident of the abilities God has given you. But, stay in a place of reliance on the Holy Spirit.

> *"No temptation has overtaken you except such as is common to man; but God is faithful, who will not allow you to be tempted beyond what you are able, but with the temptation will also make the way of escape, that you may be able to bear it." (vs 13)*

Temptation came to Jesus. Temptation will come your way, too We are not helpless against temptation. For that matter, nothing can come that must overwhelm us.

One of the keys to overcoming temptation is not to place oneself in a position to fail. "The LORD shall preserve you from all evil; He shall preserve your soul," (Psalm 121:7).

The Holy Spirit seals the believer. Even so, we may still be tempted by sin. The good news is that this preservation can keep us from sin. Yes, I do still sin. But my lifestyle is not that of one who lives a sinful life.

> *"The LORD shall preserve your going out and your coming in. From this time forth, and even forevermore," (Psalm 121:8).*

Wherever you may roam in life, the Holy Spirit promises protection.

> *"I will lift up my eyes to the hills—From whence comes my help?" (Psalm 121:1).*

King David lifted his eyes toward Mount Zion. Places are important to God. David's focus was upon the Holy place. Right things happen in right places. If I were not a pastor, I would still be a regular church attender.

> *"My help comes from the LORD, Who made heaven and earth," (Vs 2).*

I feel as if I should not have to say this, but...

Our focus is not to be upon the church, but upon the Lord of the Church.

> *"He will not allow your foot to be moved; He who keeps you will not slumber," (Psalm 121:3).*

Life can deal us some blows. But our feet do not have to be moved from the rock. My life is built upon revelation knowledge of the Word of God. I will not be moved away from His best nor lose my focus upon Him.

"Behold, He who keeps Israel shall neither slumber nor sleep," (Psalm 121:4).

Rest well today.

Your God is not asleep.

For that matter, He is not even sleepy.

"The LORD shall preserve your going out and your coming in. From this time forth, and even forever-more." (PSALM 121:8)

CHAPTER 20

"Back Talk"

I'm a Negotiator.

I have always wanted my way.

"Don't back talk me," Mom would roar.

"You had better button that lip, boy," Granny Blum often said.

Mrs. Edith Reed was my 5th grade teacher. She tired of my "negotiation" and sent me to the principal's office. The principal was Mr. Archie Reed. Amazingly, "Old Lady Reed" had a son.

He read the report and asked for my side of the story. I angrily told him I had no idea how she could reach such an unjust conclusion.

"I will brook no such insolence," he sternly stated.

I learned two things:

1. Don't irritate the principal's mom
2. The word "brook" can be used both as a verb and an object in the same sentence.

"You're snared by the words of your mouth," (Proverbs 6:2).

Consider the alternative, "Every word of God is pure," (Proverbs 30:5).

Life is one long learning experience. I'm glad I have another day to learn. I'll learn something tomorrow, too.

I'll choose my focus again.

The things of the Spirit.

And His Word.

CHAPTER 21

Doing Our Part

I Fell Off a Horse

I was riding behind my cousin, Nell.

We started up a steep hill and I fell over backward. Nell attempted to help me back up on the horse, but couldn't.

I still remember her saying, "Malc, you will have to do your part for this to work." I "did my part", we got back on the horse and made it safely home.

My part was more than just expecting Nell to lift me back into place. I had to help pull myself back up.

In spiritual things, we must supply our part.

Speaking in love, Paul told the Ephesians to do their part.

> "...But, speaking the truth in love, may grow up in all things into Him who is the head—Christ— **16** from whom the whole body, joined and knit together by what every joint supplies, according to the effective working by which every part does its share, causes growth of the body for the edifying of itself in love," (Ephesians 4:15-16).

Every member of the Body of Christ has something to supply.

The one way in which we are all equal is we're given 24 hours each day.

Another is that each of us has been given an individual measure of faith:

> *"For I say, through the grace given to me, to everyone who is among you, not to think of himself more highly than he ought to think, but to think soberly, as God has dealt to each one a measure of faith," (Romans 12:3)*

Smith Wigglesworth was a legendary British Evangelist.

He was known for bold faith and supernatural understanding of Scripture.

Seven Abiding Truths Wigglesworth Lived By

1). Bring your mind to the Word of God.

2). Don't bring the Word of God to your mind.

3). Evident faith is produced by investing time in the Word of God.

4). Examine yourself to see if you are in the faith, or just talking faith.

5). Divine Order is produced by soaking oneself in the Word and Spirit.

6). Wise believers pray short prayers in public, but long ones when alone.

7). Faith doesn't take any strength to carry, it carries you.

I'm especially drawn to points four and seven.

There is a clear difference between living by faith and "talking" faith.

Faith never takes anything from us, but adds to our daily lives.

Believers add faith to faith by studying the Word of God.

You can see a measureable difference in your life.

Start by implementing Wigglesworth's steps today.

"Do your part by getting back on the horse and trying again,"

—MALC BURTON

CHAPTER 22

Avoid Disrespecting Others Today

We All Have Buttons.

Things others do that upset us.

My only real "hot button" is disrespect.

The problem is that button can be easily pushed.

I grew up in rural Texas in a Pentecostal home. My father was not a real "church goer", but Mom was devout.
Yet, they had one thing in common: They gave me a clear understanding that I should avoid disrespecting others.

"Your light is never made to burn brighter by turning someone else's light off," ---John Osteen.

John Osteen, founding pastor of Lakewood Church in Houston, Texas, was a remarkable man of faith.
He changed my life when I heard him speak to someone about the failure of another man of God.
He gently rebuked the critic, "Brother, you are old enough to be the man's father. If your son had failed in a similar way, how would you feel about someone speaking of your son as you just did about their son?"
The man "got the point" and moved on from the conversation.

When I was about 12 I said something disrespectful about a

classmate I suspected of speaking against me.

Granny Blum, my maternal grandmother, was a genius and master of "pithy" commentary.

"So," she said, "you don't really know if this boy has said anything against you, right?"

I grudgingly admitted that I had no such knowledge, but I really thought it was probably so.

Once again, Granny said something amazing. "Malcolm Gene, life is not all about you. It's pretty unlikely people are really spending very much time conspiring against you. They're too busy trying to live their own lives."

I took Granny's advice.

I made an effort to befriend the boy.

Over time we became lifelong friends.

> *"The godly of the land are my heroes. I will invite them into my home," (Psalm 16:2).*

I'm thankful for the friendships I have.

I'm especially appreciative for my Christian friendships.

I agree with King David. "The godly of the land are my heroes."

Those are the people in whom I choose to invest most of my time.

Maybe, like me then, you could benefit from refocusing your attention.

Disrespect is a seed best never sown.

Consider this truth: "The kindest word is an unkind word unsaid."

CHAPTER 23

Five Things I Know for Certain

I am Not a Questioning Christian.

I do not cling to faith while harboring unbelief.

I believe the Word of God and will not be moved off it.

Oh yes, I have things I do not understand. But, I believe the Word of God.

There are a great many things I believe. Let me put forth five truths I gleaned from my morning Bible reading.

1) The Deepest Parts of Me Long to Intimately Know God.
"Out of the depths I have cried to You, O LORD; 2 Lord, hear my voice! Let Your ears be attentive to the voice of my supplications," (Psalm 130:1-2).

I am not a shallow person. I cannot be satisfied with shallow Christianity. I am a "whole hog or nothing, in or out" sort of believer.

I want every day to be an experience with the God of the Bible. The pathway to this place in God requires me to choose a deeper walk with the Lord each day.

2) My Past Sins Really Are Forgiven.
"If You, LORD, should mark iniquities, O Lord, who could stand? 4 But there is forgiveness with You, That You may be feared," (Vss 3-4).

I am not in sin today. But, I have committed big-time sin in the past. I am forgiven today because of a Big-Time Savior. So, I refuse to hold others in their past place of failure. I have no intention of living in my own past place of failure.

My past sins really are forgiven...*and I choose to live in forgiveness today.*

3) I Am as Certain That God Will Do Great Things for Me as I Am That Morning Follows Night.

> *"I wait for the LORD, my soul waits, and in His word I do hope. 6 My soul waits for the Lord More than those who watch for the morning. Yes, more than those who watch for the morning," (Vss 5-6)*

I have stood watch over calamity. I have stayed awake all night mourning. When my Mom died, I stayed awake most of the night. My heart was screaming out in pain, but I had made a promise. My promise to Mom was that I would "be happy" and celebrate her life.

Because of relationship issues, I know what it is like to literally weep all night while walking around my home. But, I have also experienced deliverance and know that the coming dawn of morning light is a certainty.

At my Mom's funeral I was able to minister with joy, comfort my family and reassure my suffering congregation of God's goodness because The Holy Spirit is deeply involved in my life.

Wipe the tears from your face. Look toward Jesus.

Daylight will manifest in your life very shortly.

I Know I Am Redeemed

> *"O Israel, hope in the LORD; For with the LORD there is mercy, and with Him is abundant redemption. 8 And He shall redeem Israel from all his iniquities," (Vss 7-8).*

I am not partially redeemed. The full price of redemption has been paid for me. God has poured out abundant redemption upon my life. I have been bought back from the captivity of both sin and iniquity. Sin can only have as much control over me as I will allow it to have.

Victorious living is a choice...*and I choose to live the life of God today.*

5) I Know the Life of God Flows Out of Me to Others

"On the last day, that great day of the feast, Jesus stood and cried out, saying, If anyone thirsts, let him come to Me and drink. 38 He who believes in Me, as the Scripture has said, out of his heart will flow rivers of living water," (John 7:37-38).

You and I know a lot of people who need to know the Lord. We know even more people who are simply hurting and need God's help. I have been called to make a difference in the earth and I choose to do so.

If you wonder where I am headed today, don't.

Wherever it is, I'll be making a difference.

Please join me in saying the same.

"I want every day to be an experience with the God of the Bible. The pathway to this place in God requires me to choose a deeper walk with the Lord each day,"

—MALC BURTON

Chapter 24

Refusing to Live in Judgment

I have faced judgment in my lifetime.
I know how badly it can hurt...*how unjust it can be.*
Because of this pain, I refuse to live in judgment of others.

> *"But with me it is a very small thing that I should be judged by you or by a human court. In fact, I do not even judge myself. 4 For I know of nothing against myself, yet I am not justified by this; but He who judges me is the Lord," (1 Corinthians 4:3-4).*

I had a strange dream one night. That particular dream drove me to pray. A tall wave of water was approaching a high school friend. She is someone I have known since first grade...over 50 years.

Until recently, I had only seen her once, when we were in our twenties and she had just graduated from nursing school. For the sake of literature, let's give her a name....*Mandy.*

That is not her name...but it is short and will do for the sake of reference.

Immediately upon graduation from high school, Mandy married a classmate. It was an awful marriage. He was a heavy drinker who routinely beat her when he had a tough day. Additionally, he was what my Granny Blum would call "a womanizer."

In the Spring of 2008, Mandy's last child graduated college. Her husband got drunk again and beat her with a vengeance.

Finally, at a breaking point and with nothing to anchor her to that geographic location, she moved out of her home.

On a hospital visit in the East Texas region, I was surprised to see Mandy in the hallway. She suddenly poured out her heartache and asked for prayer...which I did as we stood there with tears flowing down her cheeks.

The worst part of Mandy's story was that, since leaving her husband, her local church had excommunicated her.

I believe what I saw in the dream was a flood tide of criticism directed toward her when she needed it the least.

You probably know someone who is overwhelmed by criticism.

Be their buffer....*standing between them and their critics.*

Be their blesser...*declaring good things over them.*

Be their intercessor...*driving back evil things.*

The Seed you Sow is the harvest you will reap.

CHAPTER 25

Five Expectations From Ruth

Ruth and Naomi Were Suffering.

Their entire family had died in a famine.

In Ruth 2, we find Ruth and Naomi in Bethlehem.

Although this was Naomi's homeland, it was a foreign land to Ruth.

Ruth followed her mother-in-law to Israel in faith that Naomi knew best. What does this have to do with us? When we follow the Lord into a foreign place out of loyalty to Him, He will provide for us as He provided for Ruth.

1. Divine Connections.
> *"So Ruth the Moabitess said to Naomi, "Please let me go to the field, and glean heads of grain after him in whose sight I may find favor," (Ruth 2:2)*

Hunger was a very real thing. So was abuse of women workers by men in the fields. Ruth happened upon the field of Boaz. This was a divine connection. Ruth could have landed in anyone's field, but the Lord ordered her steps to one of Naomi's family members.

2. Divine Strategies
> *"Then Boaz said to Ruth, "You will listen, my daughter, will you not? Do not go to glean in another field, nor go from here, but stay close by my young women. 9 Let your eyes be on the field which they reap, and go after them," (Ruth 2:8-9A)*

Boaz took notice of Ruth and gave her a strategy. Following a Divine strategy will produce Divine results.

"Listen, my daughter. Do not go to glean in another field and leave this one. Stay close to my young women. Keep your eyes on the field in which they reap and follow after them."

3. Divine Protection

"I have commanded the men not to touch you. When you are thirsty, go to the vessels and drink from what the young men have drawn," (Ruth 2:9b).

Boaz was giving an instruction of protection.

As I just noted, the workplace could be dangerous for a woman.

Boaz was a man with "clout". The words he spoke mattered, especially the words of favor, blessing and protection he spoke over Ruth.

4. Divine Favor

'So she fell on her face, bowed down to the ground, and said to him, 'Why have I found favor in your eyes, that you should acknowledge me, a foreigner?'" (Ruth 2:10).

Ruth's reputation created favor in the community. Ruth responded to Boaz with thanksgiving for Divine Favor. Thanksgiving will keep the River of God's Favor flowing in your life.

Boaz answered and said to her, "I have been told all that you have done for your mother-in-law after the death of your husband, and how you left your father and mother and your homeland and came to a people you did not know before. May the Lord reward your deeds. May you have a full reward from the Lord, the God of Israel, under whose wings you have come to take refuge" (Ruth 2:10-12).

5. Divine Harvest

Ruth was willing to work. We must be willing to work, too. But Ruth's Divine Connection and Divine Favor led to a Divine Harvest.

> "When she got up to glean, Boaz commanded his young men, 'Let her glean even among the bundles, and do not harm her. Also pull out some grain for her from the bundles and leave (handfuls on purpose) so that she may glean it, and do not rebuke her,'" (Ruth 2:15-16).

Ruth's favor came from right alignment.

It's time to make sure we're properly aligned.

Being incorrectly aligned will hinder our harvest.

"Boaz took notice of Ruth and gave her a strategy. Following a Divine strategy will produce Divine results,"

—MALC BURTON

CHAPTER 26

Am I Making a Difference?

Alex Was a Missionary.

He spent decades "plowing" hard soil.
He spent more than 40 years in Southeast Asia.
Alex started churches that, honestly, did not seem to flourish.
He trained leaders in Japan, China, Vietnam, Laos and Cambodia.

Alex died satisfied that he had done his best and saw some of the results of his labor. But, honestly, the results Alex saw then are nothing compared to the harvest of today. All of Asia is exploding with a powerful move of God born of the seed sown by Alex and others.

During deep times of reflection, Alex wondered if the years of enduring hostility and rearing his children in a foreign culture had really mattered.

"Those who sow in tears shall reap in joy," (Psalm 125:5)

Alex confided to me that he "wondered." Questions arose after returning to the US and living a life of honor. He held a full professorship in a university and was a respected teacher. The times of fellowship we had while we served together on the faculty are among the highlights of my clearly blessed lifetime.

Yet, when he went to bed and turned off the lights, before entering sleep, the tormenting questions came to this amazing man of God.

By any objective standard, Alex had been a difference maker.

Yet, the nagging thoughts remained.

> *"He who continually goes forth weeping, bearing seed for sowing," (Psalm 125:6A).*

Granny's Revelation

Granny Blum walked and prayed aloud.

I recall Granny praying that her family would be used of God. She would pray as she did her "chores." During the night she would walk the yard and, later, the hallway praying. Tears would often flow down her cheeks as intercession crossed her lips. "I have sown in tears, and I will reap in joy!"

As a boy I was both impressed and wearied by this type activity because I had long before tired of everything seeming to be so emotion driven.

Thank God for the Holy Spirit. He is our Supernatural Revealer. I'm thankful for Granny again as I write. Many times during my dark days I found myself walking the floor in the small apartment at Living Truth Church shouting at the top of my voice, "I have sown in tears, but I will reap in joy!"

The Repeated Question of My Life

> *"Shall doubtless come again with rejoicing, bringing his sheaves with him," (Psalm 125:6C)*

Now, I get part of the unspoken question posed in prayer. Am I making a difference? Will my efforts produce results? Candidly, this can be a tormenting thought. It must be dealt with.

Some parents read this and wonder about their efforts with their children.

I have a number of Pastors who read my work and have their own wondering.

Distill it all and we are asking, "Am I making a difference? Will I see my desired result?" The answer here is a simple one, "Yes, you are making a difference. Your labor is not in vain."

If you are in a tearful place today, joy will return to your life. You will have a harvest to present to the Lord...*and He will have a crown of reward for you.*

Conversations with my inestimably spiritual Granny Blum produced my own shorthand interpretation of this verse. "Those who sow in tears will reap in joy and see the great results of their labor."

Please choose to live in peace today.

Do not allow the evil one to steal the joy of Jesus from you.

You're a productive child and your efforts in the Kingdom are not in vain.

You will see the results your heart longs to produce.

"Am I making a difference? Will my efforts produce results? Candidly, this can be a tormenting thought. It must be dealt with,"

—Malc Burton

CHAPTER 27

Too Many Crippled Children

I'm a Country Boy at Heart.

I Live in Madisonville, Texas.
I grew up in Plum Grove, Texas.
Even so, the farming, ranching and oilfield culture is familiar to me. Yet, I'd been away from it for a very long time of living in The Woodlands.

Upon returning to "Small Town Texas" I immediately noticed the number of people who walked with a limp. It is painfully common to see people with one shoulder lower than the other. Many simply have worn out their bodies trying to make a living.

I was having lunch one Friday, Chicken Spaghetti. I was savoring the food when I noticed a man shuffling across the room. The restauranteur called the man by name and asked, "How are things at your ranch?"

No one had to tell me. He was most likely another person injured or worn out by hard ranch work.

> *"Jonathan, Saul's son, had a son who was lame in his feet. He was five years old when the news about Saul and Jonathan came from Jezreel; and his nurse took him up and fled. And it happened, as she made haste to flee, that he fell and became lame. His name was Mephibosheth,"* (2 Samuel 4:4).

Mephibosheth.

He Was Dropped at Age Five.

The son of Jonathan, he was the grandson of King Saul. News came that his father and the king had been killed by the Philistines in a battle at Mt. Gilboa. In those days when a king was deposed the lineage was killed off.

Incorrectly supposing that David had killed King Saul, Jewish history teaches the nurse maid ran with Mephibosheth in an attempt to escape and take him somewhere safe.

As you read above, while trying to help, she dropped him. He is thought to have suffered neurological damage, and the function of his feet and legs were never quite the same.

Time passed by, but David never lost his love for Jonathan, Mephibosheth's father, who had been his best friend. David asked his primary servant, Ziba, if any of Jonathan's family still lived. David said, "I want to show them the kindness of God."

Ziba said, "There is one, a boy named Mephiobsheth, but he can't walk."

> *King David sent for Mephibosheth. "And Mephibosh eth the son of Jonathan, son of Saul, came to David and fell on his face and paid homage. And David said, "Mephibosheth!" And he answered, "Behold, I am your servant." 7 And David said to him, "Do not fear, for I will show you kindness for the sake of your father Jonathan, and I will restore to you all the land of Saul your father, and you shall eat at my table always." 8 And he paid homage and said, "What is your servant, that you should show regard for a dead dog such as I?" (2 Samuel 9:6-8).*

Mephibosheth was of royal lineage, yet we can see from this passage he had a bad self-image. All believers are of the royal family, yet many of us have a bad self-image.

Maybe You Did Something Wrong

Maybe you're suffering because of personal wrongdoing. I have things that are still hurting me because of my wrongdoing. I wronged someone, they wronged me in return, and the pain is still there. I'm better than I was and determined to get completely healed because I believe that is the will of God for my life...*and for yours, too.*

It May Not Be Your Fault

Bad things happen.
Bad things happen to good people.
Even the righteous have had bad things happen to them.
Maybe somebody dropped you. Maybe you tripped over something. Maybe you tripped over someone. Whatever the case, you tripped.

Multitudes Too Many

No matter how it happened, there are too many hurting today. Some people are suffering because of things that happened in the world. Sadly, some people are suffering because of things that have happened to them in church.

We May Need to Change
• Our self-perception.
• Our expectations.
• Our confession.

Negative self-perceptions must go.

"This is just how I am." Unacceptable.

"All the men in my family die before age 50." Unacceptable.

"There is no one on earth who wants to marry me." Unacceptable.

Alternate Faith Declarations

"I want to be better."

"Change is probably necessary."

"I am willing to what is needed to change my outcome."

"I plan to live a long, healthy, productive life."

"God has someone who is perfect for me."

Words are Quite Important

Words create atmospheres.

Work on your atmosphere.

State your heart desires.

Not just what you feel.

You'll be amazed.

CHAPTER 28

From the Holocaust to Happiness

Corrie Ten Boom.

Corrie is a modern legend.
She survived The Holocaust.
The Hollander hid fleeing Jews.
She was imprisoned in Ravensbruck.
Her sister, Betsie, died there December 16, 1944.

14 days later, Corrie was released. The next day, December 31, 1944, all the women in her age group were executed.
Historians claim her exodus was due to "...a clerical error."
After the war concluded, she returned to Germany and preached everywhere doors opened for her. She spoke passionately of the need to not just receive, but also extend God's forgiveness.

In Munich, she saw someone familiar. He was wearing a long black leather coat. The removed death's head skull remained outlined on the leather.

He was one of the SS guards at the shower room. The man was one of the Nazis who taunted the women who were forced to disrobe before showering. Corrie remembered her sister shivering from the cold and the crudity of the statements made by the guards.

Remarkably candid, Corrie wrote, "I had murdered him at least 1000 times in my heart."

That Munich morning had been a powerful one in the realm of the Spirit. Corrie had preached from Romans 5:8, "But God commends (proves) His love towards us, in that while we were yet sinners, Christ died for us."

She tried to avoid the Nazi, but he lingered. Finally there was no choice but to walk his direction.

While extending his hand the former SS member smiled broadly, bowed and said, "How grateful I am for your message, fraulein. Isn't it wonderful to know all our sins and evil deeds have been covered by His blood?"

"I, who had preached so often the need to forgive, kept my hand at my side. Even as the angry, vengeful thoughts boiled through me, I saw the sin of them."

Jesus Christ had died for this man; was I going to ask for more?

"Lord Jesus," I prayed, "forgive me and help me to forgive him." I tried to smile, I struggled to raise my hand. I could not. I felt nothing, not the slightest spark of warmth or charity.

"So again I breathed a silent prayer. 'Jesus,' I prayed, 'I cannot forgive him. Give me Your forgiveness.'

"As I took his hand the most incredible thing happened. From my shoulder along my arm and through my hand a current seemed to pass from me to him, while into my heart sprang a love for this stranger that almost overwhelmed me.

"So I discovered that it is not on our forgiveness any more than on our goodness that the world's healing hinges, but on His. When He tells us to love our enemies, He gives, along with the command, the love itself." —Excerpted from The Hiding Place, by Corrie Ten Boom.

There will probably always be someone we need to forgive. No, they may not deserve forgiveness, or even desire it. Forgive them anyway. Not just for their sake alone. Do it out of honor for our Lord.

There is no downside here.

His elevator only goes up.

The door is open.

In her amazing book, "The Hiding Place",
Corrie Tenboom recalled a particular
Nazi prison guard who had tormented
the female prisoners of the Ravensbruck
Concentration Camp. He showed up at
one of her church services in Munich.
Remarkably candid, Corrie wrote,

"I had murdered him at least 1000
times in my heart."

Yet, she forgave him because Jesus
had forgiven her.

CHAPTER 29

The Messenger –vs– The Message

You Matter.

Your message matters.

Lives will be changed by your message.

So, it is clear that the messenger is important.

Yet, the messenger is never more important than the message.

Evangelist Billy Graham lived his life without scandal. Untold millions came into the Kingdom because of his work. Yet, Dr. Graham would be the first to say the message was more important than the messenger.

Moses Was a Great Man

Moses was trusted by God to deliver The Law. The Law was quite successful in pointing us to grace.

> *"For the Law was given through Moses, but grace and truth came through Jesus Christ," (John 1:17).*

The so-called Law of Moses was not His own. Yet, Jesus epitomized, was and is, grace and truth. The principle holds: Even in the case of Jesus, The Living Word, the message was superior to the messenger. As a result of His submission to the requirements of His assignment, Jesus is exalted today.

"That (submission) is why God has now lifted Him so high, and has given Him the Name beyond all names,"
(Philippians 2:9; J.B. Phillips Translation; Parenthetical)

Submission Raises Us Higher

Maybe you could use a lift.

Jesus was lifted by submission.

I'm sure that will work for you, too.

Let's keep The Message above the messenger.

When we do so our promotion is certain.

CHAPTER 30

Things Unseen

I was upgraded.

Jeff Taylor and I had been in Nepal.

For reasons of favor, Jeff and I were in First Class.

My seat mate on the aisle was a young lawyer, a Hindu female.

Jeff was going on home to Atlanta from Mumbai, India while I had another 10 days scheduled in Bangalore, India.

A Kingdom Moment

Very tired, I closed my eyes and began to pray quietly.

Thinking I was asleep the young lawyer shook my arm. "Sir, you are speaking to someone who is not here."

"No, I said softly, "I'm speaking to someone You can't see."

This opened a witnessing opportunity that would not likely have happened any other way.

Prayer Opens Realms for Us

Prayer is a big thing.
It is both simple and complex.

Because we always need answers, prayer is essential. Each time we pray we have an opportunity to see into the Spirit realm and thereby formulate answers.

> *"For we are looking all the time not at the visible things but at the invisible. The visible things are transitory: it is the invisible things that are really permanent," (2 Corinthians 4:18).*

Visible things are short term. Invisible things offer eternal wealth beyond measure.

Keep looking by faith until you see.

CHAPTER 31

Destined to...Last

They Tied for Last.

They attended a prestigious school.

Both graduated from The Pasadena Playhouse.

Their classmates voted actors Gene Hackman and Dustin Hoffman "Least Likely To Succeed."

The superstars laugh about it now, but it wasn't funny back then.

Few of us have had the success of the two Academy Award winners. However, I'm certain we've had days when we felt nominated for the title of "Least Likely To Succeed."

I love four part harmony. My roots are deep in Southern Gospel Music. My childhood desire was to sing lead for a "name" group.

At age 17 I had a stint with The Statesmen. At age 18 I had an equally brief time with The Blackwood Brothers. Heart attacks by vocalists gave me three opportunities of about eight weeks each.

Then my dream job came open as lead singer for Mid-South. On the application, I listed my pastor as a reference. Seeing the manager of the group speaking to my pastor at a concert, I stupidly eavesdropped.

"Malc is a super guy, great singer, and a real showman, but he is not spiritual and he won't stick with you. He'll be gone before you use all the promo pictures," my pastor said.

I was crushed.

"Least Likely To Succeed" seemed to fit.

Yet, in that moment, The Holy Spirit reassured me.

The manager of the group called out to me, "Can we speak?" My heart shouted when he said, "You're our first choice for this position, you were all along. Will you join us?"

I lasted through five plus years and four record companies before we signed with Sony. Then I moved on to my true love, pulpit ministry.

> *"My thoughts are nothing like your thoughts," says the Lord. "And my ways are far beyond anything you can imagine," (Isaiah 55:8).*

For the record, we used up multiple sets of promo pictures.

"Least Likely To Succeed"? That does not describe you.

Act in faith. Schedule your promo pics today.